Llamas

By Laura Buller

Editors Sally Beets, Abhijit Dutta
US Senior Editor Shannon Beatty
Senior Art Editor Fiona Macdonald
Art Editor Mohd Zishan
Jacket Coordinator Issy Walsh
Jacket Designer Dheeraj Arora
DTP Designers Mohammad Rizwan, Dheeraj Singh
Picture Researcher Aditya Katyal
Producer, Pre-Production Dragana Puvacic
Producer Basia Ossowska
Managing Editors Laura Gilbert, Monica Saigal
Deputy Managing Art Editor Ivy Sengupta
Managing Art Editor Diane Peyton Jones
Delhi Team Head Malavika Talukder
Creative Director Helen Senior
Publishing Director Sarah Larter

Reading Consultant Linda Gambrell Ph.D.
Subject Consultant Caroline Pembro

First American Edition, 2019
Published in the United States by DK Publishing
1450 Broadway, Suite 801, New York, New York 10018
Copyright © 2019 Dorling Kindersley Limited
DK, a Division of Penguin Random House LLC
19 20 21 22 23 10 9 8 7 6 5 4 3 2 1
001–314174–July/2019

A catalog record for this book is available from the Library of Congress.
ISBN: 978-1-4654-8142-9 (Paperback)
ISBN: 978-1-4654-8428-4 (Hardcover)

DK books are available at special discounts when purchased in bulk for sales promotions,
premiums, fund-raising, or educational use. For details, contact: DK Publishing Special Markets,
1450 Broadway, Suite 801, New York, New York 10018
SpecialSales@dk.com
Printed and bound in China

The publisher would like to thank the following for their kind permission to reproduce their photographs:
(Key: a-above; b-below/bottom; c-center; f-far; l-left; r-right; t-top)

1 Getty Images: The Image Bank / Kathrin Ziegler. **3 iStockphoto.com:** thinair28 / E2. **5 Getty Images:** Karol Kozlowski / AWL Images. **6-7 Dreamstime.com:** Vaclav Volrab. **8 Dreamstime.com:** Maradt. **9 Getty Images:** Erika Skogg / National Geographic Magazines. **10 iStockphoto. com:** elisalocci. **11 Alamy Stock Photo:** Anthony Collins (c). **Dreamstime.com:** Patricio Hidalgo (t). **12-13 Alamy Stock Photo:** Arco / G. Lacz (b). **13 Getty Images:** Tim Graham / Contributor (c). **15 Dreamstime.com:** Donyanedomam. **16-17 Reyaz Limalia:reway2007-https://www.flickr.co photos/reway2007/:** https://www.flickr.com/photos/reway2007/3673061536. **18-19 Getty Images:** Steven Clarke / 500px. **20 Dreamstime.co** Pablo Hidalgo (clb); Smallredgirl (bc). **21 Dreamstime.com:** Galyna Andrushko (c); Donyanedomam (ca); Antonella865 (b). **24-25 Dreamstime.co** Izabela 23 (b). **25 iStockphoto.com:** Subbotsky (c). **26 Dorling Kindersley:** University of Pennsylvania Museum of Archaeology and Anthropolog **28-29 iStockphoto.com:** wanderluster / E+. **31 iStockphoto.com:** hadynyah / E+. **32-33 Getty Images:** Elise King / EyeEm (t). **33 Alamy Stock Photo:** dbimages / Jeremy Graham (cb). **34 Dreamstime.com:** Emicristea (bc); Laura Facchini (cl); Gábor Kovács (crb). **35 Dreamstime.com:** Bigjohn3650 (c); Eugene F (bl); Liliia Khuzhakhmetova (br). **36 Dreamstime.com:** Edurivero (bl). **36-37 Dreamstime.com:** Timbphotography (bc **37 Dreamstime.com:** Iakov Filimonov (br). **38 Dreamstime.com:** Dmitry Pichugin. **38-39 Dreamstime.com:** Bennymarty (c). **39 Dreamstime.co** Dana Kenneth Johnson (bc). **40 Depositphotos Inc:** Nyker. **41 Dreamstime.com:** Yurasova. **42 Depositphotos Inc:** DennisJacobsen (clb). **Getty Images:** Bruno Maia / 500px (crb). **43 Depositphotos Inc:** EBFoto (t). **Dreamstime.com:** Lanette63 (cla). **Getty Images:** gnes Pabar / EyeEm (crb

Endpapers: *Front and Back:* **Dreamstime.com:** Vaclav Volrab

Cover images: *Front:* **iStockphoto.com:** EJJohnsonPhotography; *Back:* **123RF.com:** Eric Isselee / isselee (cla)

All other images © Dorling Kindersley
For further information see: www.dkimages.com

A WORLD OF IDEAS:
SEE ALL THERE IS TO KNOW

www.dk.com

Contents

Chapter 1
Llama life

What's that fleecy creature peeking at you with its big eyes? Say hello to a llama. These odd-looking animals are smart and gentle mammals. They were domesticated (tamed) about 5,000 years ago in the mountains of South America. Llamas make great helpers and pets.

Llamas are related to camels. They look similar, but llamas don't have humps. Long necks stretch from their sturdy bodies.

Banana-shaped ears and large eyes give them friendly faces. Their coats are made of strong, soft fleece. Llama fleece comes in lots of colors.

Llamas love company, so they stick together. They look out for each other, especially when a baby is on the way. A baby grows inside its mom for 11 months. On its birthday, the newborn, called a cria, can wobble and walk in just an hour!

A baby llama, or cria

A herd is mostly made up of female llamas and their young.

A female llama feeds her cria milk until it can eat grass by itself.

Young llamas, or crias

Miniature llamas

Cute, miniature llamas might look like crias, but they're not. They stay small even when fully grown.

The young llamas will grow up in a herd. A llama herd is often a group of females protected by several males.

Males grow six fighting teeth. They use these to snap at each other. Mostly, though, llamas do get along.

Their fighting teeth are very sharp.

Chapter 2
What are llamas like?

Llamas are smart and friendly. They have been useful to people for thousands of years. People can train llamas in all sorts of ways. One reason people work with llamas is that they don't smell as bad as some other animals. Even their poop doesn't stink that much.

Llamas make good companions.

Llamas are famous for spitting, but they actually hate to do it. They only spit when they are very angry with another llama.

Their chins go up and ears go back as a warning before they spit. This is sometimes followed by a spray of stinky green juice.

Smelly green juice is only sprayed if the first spit is ignored by the other llama.

The llama's wild relatives lived up in the mountains. Llamas are great climbers. They have soft, padded feet to carry them over rocky surfaces. Long necks help to balance their bodies as they climb.

Their thick fleeces
help llamas to survive
in cold mountains.

Home of the llamas

For thousands of years, llamas have lived in the Andes and other mountains of western South America.

Ecuador

Ecuador
This llama is in front of Imbabura, an inactive volcano.

Peru

Bolivia

Chile

Argentina

Bolivia
The llama is Bolivia's national animal.

Peru
Llamas carried materials to help build Machu Picchu, an old city in Peru.

Argentina
Llamas are very important to Argentinian culture.

Chile
This llama is in the Atacama Desert, Chile.

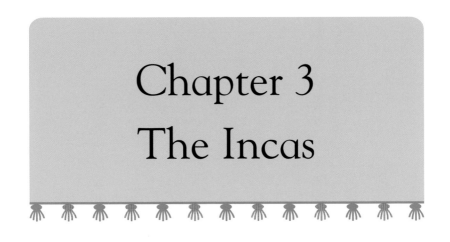

Chapter 3
The Incas

The Inca people lived in Peru from around the 12th century. They built a powerful empire, partly thanks to their animal partners.

Llamas carried heavy loads along mountain pathways. The Incas used their wool to make cloth. Llama milk was a handy drink. Their meat fed many people.

Inca farmers used llamas to carry their produce.

The Incas ruled a massive kingdom. Llamas helped to build it. Getting supplies up a mountain is not easy.

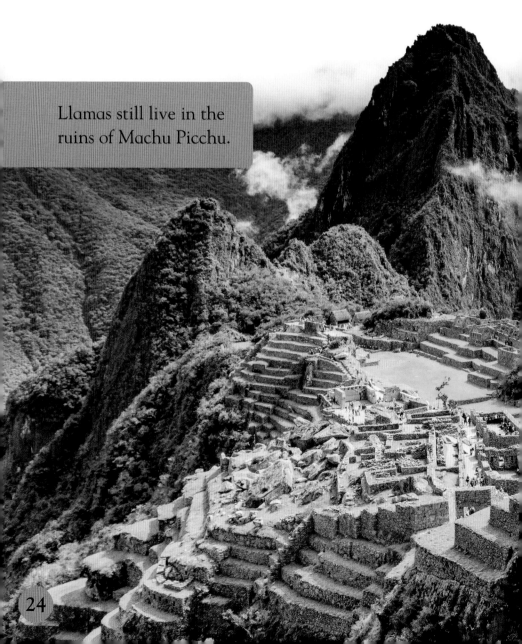

Llamas still live in the ruins of Machu Picchu.

Loaded-up llamas took materials to the site of the amazing ancient city of Machu Picchu.

The Incas knew how amazing their llama friends were. They treated them well. There are lots of llamas in their art. Inca folk stories also feature them. Some llamas in these tales can talk.

A gold Inca statue of a llama

This painting of a market scene shows the key role llamas played in Inca life.

Chapter 4
A helpful animal

Today, llamas are still helping out and making people happy. Llama-trekking is popular across the world.

Llamas aren't built for people to be able to ride them. They will happily carry bags for people, though, as they walk together.

Llama-trekking gives people a chance to interact with these friendly animals.

A woman weaving
with llama wool.

People continue to weave llama wool into cloth. Llama-wool rugs, bags, coats, and blankets can be expensive, but they last a long time.

A girl wearing traditional Peruvian clothing made from llama wool.

Some llamas have an important job on the farm. They guard other animals from attack. It takes a special kind of llama to protect other animals. Many are too shy.

A llama protecting a herd of sheep.

Llamas get along well with other animals.

The family tree

Meet the camelid family. There are three main groups: the Lama, the Vicugna, and the Camelus.

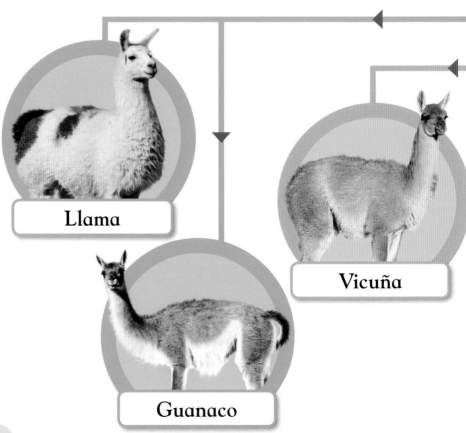

Llama

Vicuña

Guanaco

Camelidae

Lama

Vicugna

Camelus

Dromedary camel

Alpaca

Bactrian camel

Chapter 5
Llama friends

Like you and your family, the llama family has similarities and differences. All the animals in the camelid family are vegetarians.

Vicuña

They have long necks. Their legs have toenails and pads instead of hooves.

Guanaco

Llama

Their upper lips are split into
two parts. They grow sharp teeth.

Bactrian camel

The differences are mostly in body size and appearance, from ear shape to fuzzy fleece.

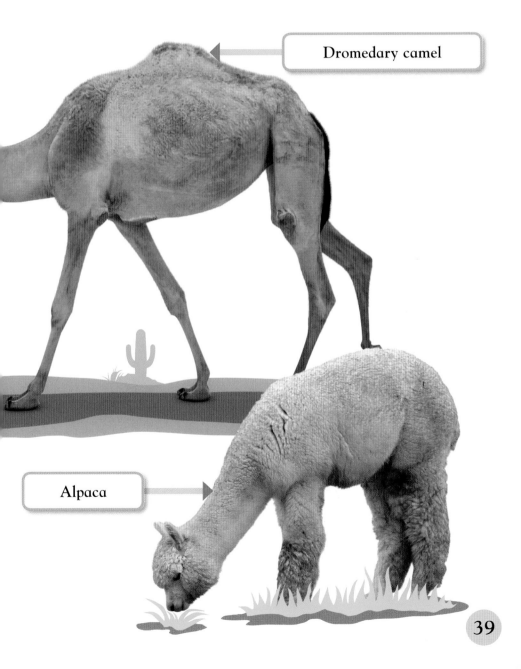

Dromedary camel

Alpaca

Alpacas look a lot like their llama cousins. How do you spot the difference? Llamas are bigger and heavier.

Llama

The alpaca has a smaller face with shorter ears. Alpacas tend to be much more fleecy, too.

Alpaca

Smile if you love llamas

Llamas express themselves with their fuzzy and sometimes silly faces. Can you make a face like a llama?

Llama fleece can be curly or straight, fine or thick.

Llamas hold their ears back if they are unhappy.

When something's not right, llamas can sound the alarm with a loud call.

Long eyelashes give llamas shade and keep out dust.

A split top lip helps llamas to reach leaves and twigs.

Quiz

 1   What South American mountains are home to many llamas?

 2   What is a baby llama called?

 3   How many fighting teeth do male llamas have?

 4   Why do llamas spit?

 5   What family are llamas a part of?

 6   Can you name the old city that llamas helped to build?

7 What do llamas have instead of hooves?

 8 What are the differences between llamas and alpacas?

 9 What things do people weave llama wool into?

 10 What job do llamas do on farms?

Glossary

camelid
any mammal that belongs to the camel family

cria
baby llama

domesticated
wild animal that has been tamed

empire
group of people or countries under one ruler

herd
large group of animals that live, eat, and move around together

Incas
South American people who built a mighty empire in Peru

Machu Picchu
ancient Inca city, built in the 15th century

vegetarian
animal that does not eat meat

Index

A LEVEL FOR EVERY READER

This book is a part of an exciting four-level reading series to support children in developing the habit of reading widely for both pleasure and information. Each book is designed to develop a child's reading skills, fluency, grammar awareness, and comprehension in order to build confidence and enjoyment when reading.

Ready for a Level 2 (Beginning to Read) book

A child should:

- be able to recognize a bank of common words quickly and be able to blend sounds together to make some words.
- be familiar with using beginner letter sounds and context clues to figure out unfamiliar words.
- sometimes correct his/her reading if it doesn't look right or make sense.
- be aware of the need for a slight pause at commas and a longer one at periods.

A valuable and shared reading experience

For many children, reading requires much effort, but adult participation can make reading both fun and easier. Here are a few tips on how to use this book with a young reader:

Check out the contents together:

- read about the book on the back cover and talk about the contents page to help heighten interest and expectation.
- discuss new or difficult words.
- chat about labels, annotations, and pictures.

Support the reader:

- give the book to the young reader to turn the pages.
- where necessary, encourage longer words to be broken into syllables, sound out each one, and then flow the syllables together; ask him/her to reread the sentence to check the meaning.
- encourage the reader to vary her/his voice as she/he reads; demonstrate how to do this if helpful.

Talk at the end of each book, or after every few pages:

- ask questions about the text and the meaning of the words used—this helps develop comprehension skills.
- read the quiz at the end of the book and encourage the reader to answer the questions, if necessary, by turning back to the relevant pages to find the answers.

Series consultant, Dr. Linda Gambrell, Distinguished Professor of Education at Clemson University, has served as President of the National Reading Conference, the College Reading Association, and the International Reading Association.